THE HEDGEHOG DIARIES OF CHARLOTTE COURT

Based on true events in our garden

April Price

DEDICATION

To all the hedgehog lovers out there..

Hedgehogs Rule

Our Hedgehogs

We love to watch our hedgehogs when they come out at night.

One, two, or maybe more, it's such an amazing sight.

Sniffing and grunting, as they go on their way,

but you shouldn't really see them out during the day.

Hedgehogs are really hard to understand, they're funny little prickly things, when they're in your hand.

If you want to help them go on their way,

Make a hole in your fence is what I would say!

Hedgehogs are in decline you know.

They're getting less and less.

So, put some food and water out.

To help them with their stress.

April Price 2018

The Hedgehog Diaries of Charlotte Court

Introduction

Our love for hedgehogs grew as we learned more about our prickly little friends.

We moved into our house in Charlotte Court during the Spring of 2015 and have always been interested in nature and all it has to give.

Every year we like to get involved counting birds and other wildlife that visit our garden. We watch the birds visiting our feeders, trees and shrubs, and make a note of what different species we see.

We also decided to have a sleep out, to try and find out what was about in our garden at night. We pitched our tent, dressed warmly and were ready for anything that might pass by!

It was uncomfortable and chilly that night, but we persevered as we were really interested to find out what was coming into our garden.

After spending hours in the tent without much luck, we decided to give up and went back into the house. We laughed about our uneventful night-watch, as our only garden visitors that night were a few cats coming over the fence now and again.

But it did make us think what actually does come alive at night in the garden while we sleep.

So we thought - camera's!

All of the hedgehogs featured in this book are wild
animals. They roam free and come and go as they please.

It is illegal to pick up a hedgehog and/or keep it as a pet.
The only time we pick up a hedgehog is to weigh it, or if
it is sick and needs to be taken to the sanctuary for
treatment.

2016

It was in 2016 that my husband Richard acquired a camera and a digital video recorder for our garden. He fixed the camera on the wall of the house, looking directly over the lawn and wired it back to the DVR and we started recording. It was fascinating and very exciting to look back at the footage from the night before.

So now instead of actually being out in the dark, losing sleep, being uncomfortable and chilly, the camera would catch anything that would pass by in our garden, at night and also during the day.

We had another camera watching three bird nesting boxes in a tree. We did observe a few blue tits peep into the nesting boxes but unfortunately they didn't decide to take up residence.

There is a family of magpies which live in a huge Leylandii tree a few doors down. They are very vocal, especially when they have babies and they make us laugh when they bring their young out for a flying lesson.

A pair of robins were caught on camera, we think they were a male and female, as one was singing a lot and the other one came to offer food. It was very sweet to watch, I guess they were a couple!

They were around for a few weeks and then just disappeared, perhaps to make a nest.

Mr and Mrs Blackbird were around the garden as well, collecting bits of twigs and coconut coir from our flower basket. It was mid-April and all the birds seemed to be wooing each other, it was very noisy with all the different kinds of bird song

Two courting robins

One day we happened to see a spotted woodpecker helping himself to the peanuts. We had never seen one here before, what a lovely sight it was and we hope he comes back regularly now that he's found our feeders. Nature is such a wonderful thing.

I remember it was a little while after having the camera when Richard played the footage back from the night before and low and behold there was a hedgehog! Our very own garden hedgehog, wow!

That marked the start of our hog watch.

I can't tell you how excited we were to know that we had a hedgehog visiting our garden.

He/she looked well fed and healthy on the camera as we watched it forage around.

We wanted to put some food and water out for the hedgehog and decided to use an upside down plastic basket, with a hole big enough for a hedgehog to go in and out, but small enough to keep the cats out and it worked.

When we looked back on the camera footage the hedgehog was visiting most nights foraging around the garden and for the food we were putting out for it. We noticed black cylindrical droppings, even in the area where it was feeding, it seems they are not fussy where they do it!

We also saw Mr Fox who came into our garden, he was very crafty. He couldn't get to the food which was underneath the basket, but decided to cunningly lift the basket off with his mouth, then he grabbed it and the basket ended up behind him on the grass.

He looked at the little basket where it fell and even gave it a shove with his leg to make sure it was out of the way.

Mr Fox

We could tell it was the same fox who was visiting most nights by its markings and it had a bit of an attitude.

After having his fill he would leave his mark, usually in the hedgehogs water bowl! We don't actually know why he did this, but I guess it's some kind of a way to make his presence known, or marking his territory.

As you can imagine he ate up all the food. It was now the early hours of the morning around 12.30am and of course when the little hedgehog came by to refill his tummy, all the food was gone!

Richard and myself sat down and had a think about what we could do next?

After all it was the hedgehogs we wanted to put the food out for.

We needed something that would keep the cats and also Mr Fox out!

We acquired a storage box with a lid and made a hole big enough for a hedgehog to go in and out, and also made a flap at the entrance.

Richard put the feeding station on top of the steps going into the garden.

We put a block on the top so it was too heavy for Mr Fox to move.

It worked! We didn't have any-more trouble from Mr Fox, although he still visited our garden on a regular basis for any scraps that he could find.

It was lovely to see Mr Fox and he looked very healthy and bushy tailed.

Whenever we cooked a chicken, we would put the carcass out on the lawn for Mr Fox and more often than not he would carry it off.

Richard decided that we needed a few more cameras,

which he put around the garden.

Let me explain the layout of our garden so that you can have a picture in your mind.

From our back door there is a patio area with three steps leading up into a lawned garden, with a few shrubs and a tree, then another three shallow wooden steps going up to what we've always called the 'dark zone'!

The 'dark zone' is a very dark and wild area of the garden that has a clematis covered pergola, an acer tree and other shrubs. Not a lot of sun gets through, hence the name.

It's a very wild place that has a log pile up against the wall. It's secluded up there and a very good place for hedgehogs. We would often see a hole in amongst the log pile and grass cuttings as if something had gone in, so that was a good sign.

It was an ideal place for a hedgehog to make its home.

Richard made some small ramps out of old pallets for the steps, as we thought that it would make life a little easier for our prickly little friends to get about more freely. As soon as the ramps were up and it got dark we didn't have to wait long before we saw a hedgehog using it to go up into the garden. That made us very happy. It meant that they could freely go to other places in the garden that they maybe had never been able to go before, as the steps were previously too deep for them.

After watching hours and hours of video footage, we
noticed two male hogs coming to blows. It was the
height of the mating season and they were letting each
other know who was boss.

We were really excited to see two hedgehogs in our
garden, even though they weren't seeing eye to eye. They
were snorting and grunting, pushing and shoving until
one ran off!

We thought that another feeding station was needed at
the bottom of the steps.

It was made in the same way as the top feeder.

The hedgehogs soon got used to using the feeding
stations, which kept the food dry when it rained,
although it seemed to be a magnet for slugs!

We had a regular hog, who at the time we think was
living under a shed two gardens away from us. We would
usually hear their dog barking and shortly afterwards we
would hear the hedgehog coming in under our fence. We
knew it was a female hog, as she was pestered by one of
the males that was coming by.

We started to call her Mrs White Spot, as when looking
back at the footage she seemed to have a white splodge
on her behind.

Richard got a plastic box and screwed it to a wooden
base, put a hole big enough for a hog to go in and out,

put some hay inside and also a little camera. This was situated in the 'dark zone'.

It wasn't long after that we saw Mrs White Spot move in and was taking leaves and other items inside to make her nest. She somehow managed to dislodge the camera which stopped working after that, maybe she was camera shy!

She was a regular visitor to the feeding stations and would come and visit, more or less at the same times every night.

After a while, we noticed a change in her behaviour, she would feed and then go straight back to her nest, which made us think that she may have babies.

We were seeing hedgehogs coming and going on a regular basis and they all had different little ways about them.

Most were really careful coming down the ramps, but there was one in particular that we noticed would just drop down the steps and seemed to be in a rush to get from A to B, which did make us laugh!

We thought that it was a male and on a mission to find a lady hog, which is exactly what he's supposed to do, mate and eat!

Some weeks went by, we didn't really count,we decided

to look at the footage yet again.

We had to laugh because watching the footage back we found it was becoming a little bit addictive.

While re-watching the footage, we happened to see a baby hedgehog!

We couldn't believe our eyes, it was a bit late in the season for baby hoglets but we've read hedgehogs can have two litters of babies. June - July time and also one later in the year.

Mrs White Spot had these babies late in the season and we knew if they didn't reach around 600g-650g before going into hibernation, they were unlikely to survive.

After spotting the baby hoglet we thought we would keep an even closer eye out for any more.

After an early work shift I came home and noticed something on the grass, it was a baby hoglet. I knew that if you see a hedgehog out in the daytime it usually means that it's not well and something is wrong. Although it is known for an adult female hedgehog to be seen in the daytime, foraging for food or water if it has babies to feed. So I picked up the hoglet very carefully and put it in a deep box with a towel, and a hot water bottle underneath the towel. I also put water and food inside and positioned it in a dark and quiet place.

I telephoned a hedgehog rescue centre, who gave me the number of our local sanctuary, they were very helpful and asked if we could bring the hoglet in for them to assess.

I messaged Richard to tell him about the hoglet. I waited until he came home from work and we went to the sanctuary together.

On the way we were saying how small he was and we named him Tiny Tim not actually knowing if the hoglet was a boy or a girl!

It was a bit of a trek to the sanctuary, but because of our love of hedgehogs and any other animals, we didn't mind how far it was.

We eventually arrived at the sanctuary and the they admitted the hoglet.

They took our name, address and telephone number and said that they would keep in touch, because they ideally wanted the hoglet to return to where it was found.

I asked if we could somehow mark the hedgehogs and hoglets and they suggested marking them with nail varnish.

That would enable us to keep an eye on them and differentiate the babies and to know how many we had coming into our garden.

Before we left they told us that the hoglet was a little boy!

On the way home we thought how appropriate the name

Tiny Tim was.

The next evening we saw another hoglet. Richard went to get it and we weighed it. It was 375g and we marked it with a little number one.

It's a good job that we did, because the next evening we saw another one which we also brought in and it weighed 475g and so we marked it with a little number two.

Another came the same night which we also weighed and this one was 325g and we marked it with a little number three.

We were by now keeping a diary of hedgehogs visiting the garden and what they weighed.

About a week or so went by and we decided to telephone the sanctuary to see how Tiny Tim was getting on. They told us that he was a little fighter, but only time would tell.

We said that we would keep in touch and mentioned that we had seen three more hoglets and would continue to keep an eye out for them.

We knew Tiny Tim was in the best place for his best chance of survival, which was very comforting to know.

In the meantime we had a lot going on in our garden with three babies to watch over!

It seemed that any spare time we had, be it early in the morning, or late at night we were watching either the camera footage live, or playing back what had already been recorded.

We decided to mark Mrs White Spot with a little W. She was a lovely mum to her babies, bringing them out when they were ready to be weaned, she taught them everything they needed to know even though they were small and vulnerable.

We even saw what the hogs do to a slug before they eat it.

They actually roll it as they walk backwards, we'd seen this behaviour on a wildlife programme but now we were witnessing it for ourselves. It was amazing to see a five week old or so hoglet doing that!

As the babies were getting bigger, Mrs White

Spot just did her own thing by going off and leaving babies one, two, and three to fend for themselves.

We would often see her just going about her business foraging in the undergrowth for food. She had done a good job by bringing her babies up.

Mrs White Spot with one of her babies

On a cold, but sunny morning, I was walking around the garden, which I did more often than not, just to check all was well before heading off to work. I walked up to the 'dark zone' and saw Mrs White Spot laying outside her nesting box, she was still.

There was no movement, she looked so peaceful just lying on the hay.

My heart felt so heavy when I realised that she had died!

It was so sad to see her just lying there.

I messaged Richard to tell him, he came home and confirmed she had passed away.

It really upset us, as we had watched her for a long time and felt we'd got to know her.

Later that evening Richard buried her in the 'dark zone'. It was a very sad day for us, but we also knew that we had an obligation to look out for her babies.

I telephoned the sanctuary and told them about Mrs White Spot and they said that perhaps she was an old hedgehog who had many babies over the years and it was just her time to go.

It was upsetting then and still is even now, as I'm writing this book.

She was a lovely mum and a very interesting hedgehog to follow on our cameras.

We miss her terribly and still think of her today.

We were seeing a few big males in our garden. They were grunting, pushing and shoving which is how we knew that they were male hedgehogs. They will fight and stand their ground, especially in the mating season.

When we were able to, we would bring the hedgehogs in and weigh them just to make sure they were well and then put them straight back outside where we had found them in the garden.

We named one Mr X (aka Fatty), he was a really big

healthy hog, who had a bit of an attitude. Half the time he would come down the steps, not using the ramps but would just flop down most of the steps and march his way down the path at the side of the house and under the gate to the front of the house. Then off he'd go for hours, but he would always come back into our garden either for food or to find a female hog, or even just to rest in one of the nesting boxes.

Other hedgehogs would come and have food and water throughout the night, I think word had got around that there was 5 star accommodation here!

Twin hedgehog nest box

Richard began his project to make a new hedgehog box out of some old pallets. It took a few days to finish but he was proud of it and we called it the bush box. He fitted a small camera inside the box so that we could see if anything would go inside, it was situated in the garden under a bush. We put some hay inside the box for bedding and waited.

We didn't have to wait long as Mr X soon took up residence. He would go out at night to forage, wander around to eat what we were putting out in our two feeding stations and look out for any female hogs that were out and about.

He would then go back into the bush box before it got light.

As there was a camera in the box we found out a few things that were unknown to us before - what male hedgehogs get up to while they're on their own. It was an eye opener and we were shocked what we were seeing to say the least.

I did check with various websites what I thought I was seeing, and it actually said he was probably having man time!

We shall just leave it at that!

Moving on swiftly…..

Richard went on to make another two hedgehog boxes which he situated up against the back wall up in the 'dark zone'.

The hogs like to forage up there and also go into the garden next door under the fence.

We had a few hedgehogs come and go in and out of the

boxes but the bush box was the one they would fight for!

One morning we were looking at the footage from the night before and saw the fox wandering around the garden, we also noticed baby number two was foraging around. We were so worried for the little hoglet when it came face to face with the fox - when I say face to face I actually mean nose to nose!

It was so close we really feared for the hoglet, as we had read that if a fox is hungry enough it will try to take a hog.

Baby number two just sat there protecting itself being very still, even after the fox had gone. The baby hoglet just stayed still for about ten minutes.

Then it just moved off and went on its way.

What a relief that was.

Wow, what we had just experienced was amazing!

Mr Fox and baby number two

There continued to be a lot of hedgehog action in our garden. Males wooing the females, circling them and following them for hours and even then the female would sometimes just walk off, or the male would get bored.

We telephoned the sanctuary to see how Tiny Tim was doing. They said that he was really well, had gone into hibernation and that we could have him back next year after hibernation, around the end of March, early April time.

The baby hoglets were thriving. We were weighing them every few weeks and they were putting on a good amount of weight, which was required for them to go into hibernation.

There was one hoglet, number three who was the smallest of them all. We named her Mini 3 she was like

Houdini. One minute we would see her, next she was gone and she went missing for a while. We had thought at one point that perhaps she hadn't made it through the cold snap that we had leading up to Christmas.

We continued to leave some food for any hedgehogs that may still be out and about before we headed off to stay with my sister, for New Year's celebrations.

By this time Richard had put our cameras online, so we could keep an eye on them when we were away from home.

On New Year's Eve night we had a quick look on our cameras and we actually saw Mini 3, she was going up the ramps. It was such a relief to see her and she was looking good.

That made our New Year even better.

But that was the last time we saw her or any other hogs!

They were all fast asleep hibernating. We had at least two in one box, and one in another.

We did always check the camera footage just in case any were about and wanting food and water, but nothing!

We had been so used to seeing a lot of hedgehog action that we felt a bit lost and sad that they had settled down for Winter.

We thought let's just hope they call by again next year.

2017

One day in January, we looked back on the footage from the night before and noticed that the gravel had been moved, but it didn't look like hedgehogs had done it. There was a lot of mess, so we were thinking maybe it was the fox. We were so shocked when we saw that it was actually a badger!

We were really surprised and at the same time horrified because a badger will eat a hedgehog. We feared for the hogs as we watched footage of the badger roaming around the garden, it went all over the garden even up the 'dark zone'. It was on a mission to find something to eat. It then went out the same way that it had come in, underneath the side gate.

It was a huge badger and looked very strong. It went up and down the steps with no problem, you could see that it was a really good size. We wouldn't have wanted to come face to face with him.

The badger

Luckily there weren't any hedgehogs in the garden that night.

Richard put a concrete block under the back gate, leaving just a hedgehog sized gap.

We didn't see the badger again.

It was very quiet in our garden now as the hedgehogs were all in hibernation. We were missing them and their antics on camera and hoping that they were all safe and sound.

We got in touch with the sanctuary, who said that Tiny Tim had woken up from hibernation and that we could come and pick him up to bring him home.

We were excited that he was coming back to our garden where he was born.

We arrived home early in the evening and Richard put Tiny Tim in the nesting box up in the 'dark zone', we hoped he would come out when it got dark, he did. He stayed around the garden for a few nights then decided to wander off and we lost track of him, but we are sure Tiny Tim is still around and about somewhere.

It was late March 2017 when we first saw one of our hedgehogs emerge from hibernation - it is amazing how they can go for such a long time without food.

Their breathing slows right down to a breath every few minutes, their body temperature drops dramatically to around 10°c or less and the heartbeat reduces. In order for the hog to come out from hibernation it's got to slowly warm it's body temperature back up, switch back on so to speak.

We started to see more and more hog activity on our cameras. They would come and eat at the food stations, forage in the garden and you could hear them go under the fence into the garden next door. We have read that male hedgehogs will travel over a mile a night, to find a female hog or for food.

We decided to get even more cameras to put up around the garden and made a few more hog boxes. Our garden was becoming even more of a hedgehog's paradise.

We were seeing more and more hedgehogs visiting to eat, or just to pass by. We counted over ten at one point. We had a few regular visitors, one who we named Mr C. He was a big hog who would often stay in one of our hog boxes, or even just a nap for a few hours in the night then move off somewhere else.

There was one hedgehog which seemed to have a tuft of spines sticking up on its head. We called it Punky. We often saw it in the bush box having a rest.

Mr C and another male, Mr X (aka Fatty) would more often than not come to blows and Mr C would normally come off the worse for wear!

A few times he ended up rolling down the steps after being pushed by Mr X. But he just waited in a ball where he landed until he knew the coast was clear to unroll and run off.

We had another big hog we called Bully, we often saw him pushing and shoving other hogs but it was full on mating season and that's what they do!
Fight for the females.
We saw a lot of wooing activity and males fighting.
But they just really want to go on their way and eat, drink and mate.

We also saw two babies. I think it was sometime in June, if I remember rightly.

We used to sit out of an evening when it was quiet and peaceful and just listen. Sometimes we could hear the hedgehogs coming, sniffling and snorting as they foraged, or even confronting another hog.

It was getting dark and I heard a noise at the side gate, that's when I saw a little hog come in, it even walked over my slipper. I just sat there still, it went past me and onto the bottom feeding station. It was feeding for about ten minutes, came out, ignored me and then just went on its way.

It's quite amazing how they know where the food is. We could usually tell if it was a new hog to our garden, as they weren't familiar with the ramps on the steps, they would look confused trying to figure out what they had to do.

A little while after, another one came in, probably from the same litter, it must have come to the feeder before, as it knew exactly where to go.

It always makes us smile when we see new hogs, it means that they are thriving in our area.

One evening we saw Mr C. We hadn't seen him for a while and thought it would be good to see how he was doing. He still seemed to be a good weight but we noticed that he was breathing noisily, so we decided we had better keep an eye on him, as we had read that hedgehogs can get lungworm.

I telephoned the sanctuary, who are always so helpful, they said the next time we see him to bring him in to be checked out if he is still in the same condition.

A few weeks passed by, we saw a few hedgehogs going about their business but not Mr C. It wasn't until a few weeks later that we saw Mr C again.

Richard went to get him to see how he was, his breathing was still bubbly and noisy, so we put him in a box with hay, food and water, put him in a dark quiet area of our kitchen and took him to the sanctuary the next day.

They asked for our name and address and telephone number the same as they did when we took Tiny Tim in. They took Mr C in and had a quick look at him and agreed that his breathing wasn't good, he also had a poorly leg, a bad eye and ringworm. They said they would take him in and they would be in touch to let us know the outcome.

We waited a few days and telephoned the sanctuary, unfortunately it wasn't good news.

Mr C was not well at all, he had a lot of health issues and whilst he was sedated and being examined they said it would be best if they put him to sleep. He would have been in a lot of pain and would suffer if left as he was.

So although we were upset at the outcome, we also knew it was the right thing to do for Mr C.

They explained to us that he had very bad deformities on his feet and wondered if it was some kind of new disease that hedgehogs could get, so they did some tests, but that didn't turn out to be the case.

They said that it looked like he had walked through something corrosive, which was very worrying for us, as hedgehogs usually cover the same ground a lot of the time.

We had got so used to seeing him and now he was gone! It was an emotional time for us both.

But we didn't lose heart as we believe Mr C has undoubtedly got siblings roaming around in our estate and that made us happy.

Shortly after losing Mr C we noticed that there were fewer hedgehogs coming for food, which made us think that they may have gone into hibernation.

We did notice one of the hedgehogs taking leaves into the bush box, it went back and forth for hours making its nest.

It's so lovely to see and encouraging to know that they feel safe enough to nest and settle in our garden.

So once again our garden was very quiet.

A hedgehog preparing for winter and hibernation

2018

The months passed and it was soon time to get ready for the return of our hedgehogs.

We began by making two new feeding stations similar to the ones they had last year.

Richard fixed them to the wall with a bungee cord to stop the fox moving them.

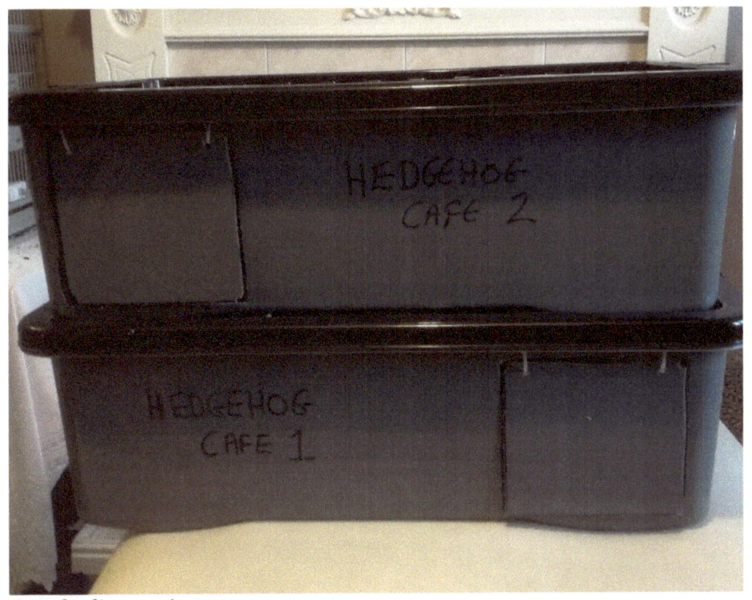

Our feeding stations.

It was around March 2018 when we first noticed a hedgehog, we called it Titch, although it was actually a very good size at 840g considering the time of year and that it may have just come out from hibernation.

Over the next few weeks we saw a few more hedgehogs which came in for food and water and at the same time I imagine looking around our garden for any female hedgehogs.

There were two male hedgehogs that we named Eric and Ernie they always seemed to cross each other's paths and have a bit of a scuffle, but we never saw anything too aggressive, it would be pushing and shoving mainly and one would just curl up, as if in surrender!

By now it was early April, a female that we named Flo was being harassed by one of the two male hogs that we've seen around the garden,

he even followed her into one of the nesting boxes where they remained for quite a while. He was wooing her and trying very hard to win her affection, eventually he got bored and just walked off leaving her alone in the box.

Flo and a male hedgehog

I have no doubt that he succeeded later as they are quite persistent.

Male hedgehogs are promiscuous and can mate with many female hedgehogs and the females also mate with different males trying to conceive. A litter of hoglets can have different fathers!

A few months passed, we were seeing a lot of hedgehogs come and go and noticed that Flo had taken up residence under a log pile up in the 'dark zone'. She was carrying mouthfuls of leaves back and forth. Although there was food readily available for her she always preferred to forage for her own.

The fox would visit from time to time and have a look around the garden for any scraps.

We saw a few more hedgehogs who we named Henry, George and Punky Two, this was around the month of June. There was lot going on in our garden at the time, so we couldn't really keep tabs on them accurately.

We were about to go on holiday to Switzerland for a week and because our local hedgehogs were so used to calling into our garden for food, we didn't want them to go without. So we left instructions for my daughters to put food and water out for them while we were away.

Even though we were hundreds of miles away enjoying our holiday, it didn't stop us from checking the cameras every now and again to see who and what was visiting our garden, we missed seeing them.

A few weeks after returning back from our holiday we saw a baby hedgehog. Richard brought it in so that we could weigh it.

It was 238g, we put two little dots on it so we could keep an eye out for it. When I went into work at our local hospital the following day, I told my work colleagues that we've had a new baby hoglet in our garden and we were looking for name suggestions. Some of my work colleagues and I were talking about some medical instruments that day and the name Rampley came up. So we decided to call it Rampley.

We often saw Flo and Rampley together, although baby Rampley would be seen foraging around the garden and Flo would just go off and leave the baby to fend for itself.

A couple of weeks later we weighed Rampley again, it had put on 100g, but we noticed that it had a lot of ticks on it. We've got a tick removal tool, it enabled Richard to get the whole tick with the head attached, off of the hedgehog.

He removed around eight ticks in total.

George was still around and calling by for food regularly and so was Flo.

As Autumn was descending upon us we were seeing less hedgehog activity in our garden.

Richard freshened up the nesting boxes with some fresh hay and collected leaves and put them around the garden and up in the 'dark zone', hoping that it would encourage the hedgehogs to use them for bedding in our garden.

The weather started to change it got very wet and windy. We were still seeing a few hedgehogs coming for food to build up their reserves for this year's hibernation, including a hedgehog we had not seen before. We decided to call it Betty, although we were not sure of its sex.

During early October I was awake around 5am as I had to go into work.

While I was having my cup of tea and looking at the live footage I saw Betty, she was so funny she peeped out of the feeding station, started to go out and then dashed back in.

I don't think she liked storm Callum very much. I continued to watch until she eventually came out a few minutes later. She speedily ran up the ramps and up into the garden had a little forage then went under the fence next door. Her nest couldn't have been that far away as it was soon to be light.

During the nights following storm Callum we saw a lot of hedgehog activity. Flo and baby Rampley had a brief encounter, then went their separate ways.

We saw at least four more hedgehogs coming to the feeders that evening: Henry; Betty; Punky Two; and a new unmarked one.

The storm passed and the weather had improved to a point where we were having some sunny days which was very welcome.

On the video we had been seeing a big hedgehog without any markings and so we knew that it was a new one that we hadn't seen before. It was coming and going in and around the garden most nights, foraging and just enjoying roaming around and then it would just disappear with no trace!

I saw Rampley a few times and thought we should weigh him just to see how he was doing. We were so glad to know he had put on a good bit of weight - 730g, enough for him to go into hibernation.

One evening the big unmarked hedgehog appeared in our garden and was coming down the ramps. Richard went out to get the hedgehog and we weighed it. He was in very good condition and a healthy weight at 1190g. We named him Houdini as no sooner as we saw him, he was gone again. We also saw Betty being bullied by another male which made us think that Betty wasn't a female hedgehog after all, so we renamed him Bertie.

We can only really guess if they are male or female from

watching their behaviour and antics, we never examine them in an intrusive way which may upset them.

One morning we were watching the footage and saw Henry taking leaves into one of the nesting boxes up in the 'dark zone'. He was collecting leaves for hours, having a bit of a rest in between. He did make us laugh as he tried to drag a branch in with him! The branch got stuck in the doorway. It was nearing 7am when he decided to go in and snuggle down for the day.

Most evenings we were seeing Flo, Rampley and Henry. One morning while looking back on the previous night's video, we caught a glimpse of what looked like a baby hoglet, wandering around the garden searching for food. It was doing a good job, spending at least an hour in our garden foraging. We decided to keep an eye out for it, as it was obviously from a late litter and in need of a bit of extra food.

The following evening we happened to see it again, it was in the garden and very close to where Henry was!

He gave the baby hoglet a bit of a nudge, but otherwise ignored it and just carried on foraging himself.

We brought the hoglet in and weighed it. It was very small at 306g but otherwise looked to be in good health. We put a little dot on it and called it Spot.

Shortly afterwards we noticed another hoglet come in from the side gate and go into the feeder, which is situated at the bottom of the steps.

When it had finished feeding we brought it in to weigh and marked it with two spots. It weighed 397g and we called it Sniffy.

Towards the end of October Mr Fox made several visits to the garden, and on one occasion had a very close encounter with Bertie.

Bertie acknowledged him, seemed a bit apprehensive at first, but decided that he wasn't going to be a threat and just carried on.

Mr Fox and Bertie

By early November we were only seeing the two new baby hoglets - Spot and Sniffy coming into the garden regularly for food and water, although they never appeared to actually meet each other.

Spot had moved into Henry's box in the 'dark-zone' but Sniffy always went out by the side gate.

We were pleased to know that they are almost at a good weight for hibernation.

It is very rewarding to see the baby hedgehogs thrive and become adults, it really touches our hearts. There are so many hedgehogs that pass through our garden now, we feel very privileged.

Just to think that it all started back in 2016 when we saw just one hedgehog.

We've been hedgehog fanatics ever since.

I've noticed on social media, that a lot of people are becoming more aware of the hedgehogs plight!

They are helping by putting food and water out for them, making homes, gaps in fences and even hedgehog highway signs.

I think that we are all becoming more aware and understanding of our hedgehogs' needs. The more we all talk about our little prickly friends, the more people will be educated.

Keep up the good work everybody.

We love our hedgehogs.

If it wasn't for our eight camera's, we wouldn't be able to watch over these hedgehogs and little hoglets in the way that we do!

SUMMERY

Ramps and feeding stations

We look forward to watching our hedgehogs again in 2019.

The death of Mr C made us think how he got his deformity. Maybe it could have been from people washing their patios with corrosive substances and not rinsing it off properly.

We will never fully know what our hedgehogs have to face, the many obstacles caused by us humans and unless we are made aware of what we could be doing to our wildlife, a lot more hedgehogs will suffer.

We did some research on the Internet to find and print out some helpful information so that we could distribute flyers around our local vicinity. We did this to make our neighbours aware that there are hedgehogs around our estate and pass on some basic information about how we can help them and encourage them to stay.

So many hedgehogs get injured whilst people are gardening with strimmer's and other gardening equipment.

We found out more and more about our prickly friends and we were really shocked and saddened to learn that they are in decline.

We need to try and change this by becoming more aware of the hedgehogs needs.

Lawned gardens and bushes are becoming a thing of the past as some people prefer outside spaces that can be easily maintained with hard standings and gravel to park cars.

If we don't stop and think about our wildlife a lot of animals will suffer.

If you would like to encourage hedgehogs into your garden make sure that you leave a small gap in your fence. A CD case sized gap so that they can travel from one garden to another.

Maybe let a small area of your garden grow wild if you can, so that they can forage. Leave some water out for them to drink, especially in the hot weather, water can be very hard for them to find.

We put chicken cat or dog food out and cat biscuits. Although they forage for their food, they do also like the additional food that we put out for them.

If possible you could set up your own camera so that you can see and enjoy what comes into your garden, sit back and relax and watch your very own nature video and, if you're lucky, even your own garden hedgehog!

I hope that you have enjoyed reading my book just as

much as we have enjoyed watching the hedgehogs over the past three years.

There have been some highs and lows and although this is the end of my book, it certainly won't be the end of our hog watching.

Special thanks to Martin Price, for our handmade hedgehog "Harold"

<u>Hedgehogs</u>

45

Hedgehogs roam around at night

If you're lucky, you may catch sight.

Spikey and prickly, with a black shiny nose

They can roll up in a ball you know!

Sniffing and snorting, foraging for food

They keep the slugs down, so that is good.

The numbers are falling, it's so sad to hear

My heart feels so heavy and I shed a tear.

So long live the hedgehog and keep them right here!

Let's all help them live and thrive with no fear.

By April Price 2018

ABOUT THE AUTHOR

April is a hard working housewife, who works for the NHS.

Her work colleagues also know her as the crazy hedgehog lady.

She has always had a love of nature and animals from a young age.

Any feedback would be kindly appreciated

email the author: april.price@sky.com

Acknowledgements

Edited by Dawn Howton. Special thanks for all of your hard work.

Thanks to Marie, Jon and Jay, Louise, Rees and Haydn for feeding the hedgehogs while we were on holiday.

Special thanks to my husband, Richard, for putting the cameras around the garden, to allow us to view the hedgehogs.

Without the recorded video footage, I wouldn't have been able to write this book.

Based on true events in our garden over a three year period.

All of the hedgehogs featured in this book are wild animals.

They roam free and come and go as they please.

It is illegal to pick up a hedgehog and keep it as a pet.

By April Price ©2018